GREEN CHILI

A COOKBOOK BY

BETTE SHANNON

TREASURE CHEST PUBLICATIONS, INC.
1850 W. GRANT ROAD., SUITE #101
PO BOX 5250
TUCSON, ARIZONA 85703

Drawings and Sketches

by

CONNIE ASCH

Design, Arrangement,

Typesetting & Editing

by:

Nancie Mahan * Leta Lyle * Ethel Branson

ISBN 0-918080-08-8

Contents

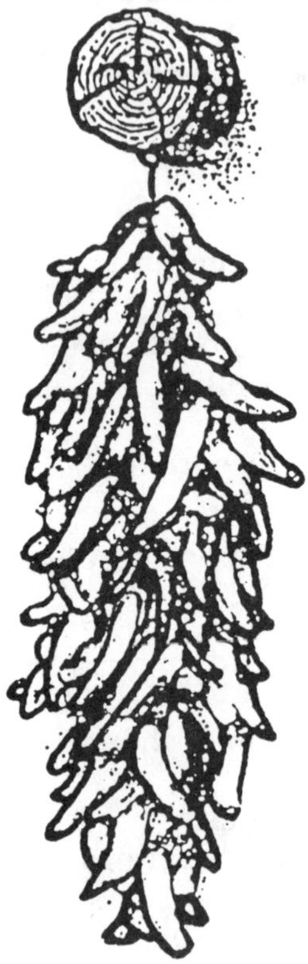

CHAPTER I

An Informal Introduction to Green Chili

"Man, that's delicious! Now, that's what I call cookin'."

Modesty being one of my less obvious attributes, I accepted the accolade. But I can't take all the credit. I have to admit that that mysterious, aromatic, pungent, little green devil I use so often in my cooking is the secret. Green Chili.

When the Spanish explored and settled in the Southwest areas of what is now our United States, they brought the plants from the south. The Indians of Mexico had taught them how to blister and peel the pretty green pods. After learning to use green chili in various dishes, the Spanish wouldn't leave home without it.

What two words do you immediately think of when someone mentions Mexican cooking? "Hot" and "chili." Or perhaps some of you think of two other words--New Mexico. Why not? The amount of acreage devoted to growing chilies in New Mexico is enormous. New Mexicans, whether Spanish-American, Indian, Anglo, or transplants from anywhere in the world, proudly display small and large ristras (those strings of red chilies which, before being dried, were green chilies) outside near the door. The vivid red of dried green chili pods makes a splash of color against the creamy tans and browns of adobe walls. When you see a ristra, you know that within lives a true Southwesterner.

Older than civilization the southwest itself, green chili has long been a staple in the diets of native New Mexicans. And for good reason! Not only is it a delicious vegetable, but it is also loaded with some of the most important vitamins necessary to our good health. Many of us are searching for ways to break out of the synthetic vitamin cycle. New Mexico State University researchers have tested and found that green chili is chock-full of vitamins A and C. They have also discovered that pods harvested in October have a higher vitamin C content than pods picked in July and August, which had shown a high C content at that time. However, heat and oxidation affect vitamin C, so if chili is dried, the vitamin C is lost. Vitamin A is practically unaffected by drying, and canned and frozen green chili retains both vitamins to the extent that in these two products the vitamin A and C content is only slightly less than in fresh green chili.*

Let's clear up one misconception first. Green chili is not an elongated Bell or sweet pepper. Green chili is a pepper of the Capsicum genus that ranges in pungency from mild to medium to hot. While the flavor of green chili can be called delicate, by no stretch of the imagination can one say green chili is sweet! Never try to eat a green chili out-of-hand as you would a Bell pepper.

A green chili that is considered mild may be too hot for some, and a green chili labeled hot may be too mild for others. Certain additions can temper the too-hot to a flicker; other additions can stoke the too-mild into a forest fire. We'll come to that a bit later.

*Cooperative Extension Service, NMSU circular 463, February 1976, New Mexico State University, Las Cruces, New Mexico 88001.

Southwestern cooks prize green chili because of its range of pungency and its unique flavor that enhances almost every dish. Cooking with green chili is an adventure because the cook must test, taste, and experiment to achieve a happy medium for her family. If the family prefers the fiery hot, the cook must again test, taste, and experiment to lower the heat for invited guests so they will not feel that steam is pouring out of their ears or that they have lost their voices as well as the linings of mouth, throat, and stomach. (As for those uninvited guests, my experiences show that they are endowed with cast iron stomachs and asbestos-lined gullets at birth. You'll have to find your own way of discouraging them. I refuse to share my method.)

Every cook I know has shelves loaded with cookbooks, boxes crammed with cards, and drawers stuffed with recipes torn out of magazines. Yet most cooks have one particular cookbook they swear by and use until death do they part. (The cookbook usually falls apart first.) So, I will assume, you have at least one favorite, basic cookbook in your kitchen. Look through your book. You'll discover that each recipe is not just a list of ingredients with instructions following. That compendium of recipes, no matter how small or how large, is a treasury of ideas. And that is really what cooking is all about—testing, tasting, and experimenting; mingling or replacing one ingredient with another; adding something that might seem utterly outrageous; presenting new tastes--yes, even failing now and then, but you'll succeed more often than not.

Once you have bought your fresh, canned, or frozen green chili, you are ready to choose one of your favorite recipes and add to it, test, taste, and experiment. Canned and frozen green chilies are ready to use; however, fresh green chili must be prepared for use. I will help you through the process of blistering and peeling the chilies, and along with a few extra pointers, I will give you a few recipes to get your ideas rolling.

In some of my recipes I have used approximate amounts because I have experimented, but I didn't always measure for accuracy as I should have. I am a firm believer in imagination and experimentation. I hope you will be innovative and have fun trying your own ideas.

CHAPTER II

Some Special Directions

Fresh green chili pods should be about 6 to 8 inches long, smooth and shiny, thick-fleshed, "broad-shouldered" (to facilitate peeling), and should taper to a blunt point. Your market may label green chilies as mild, medium, or hot. If not, check with the produce manager. In any event, after a little experience, most people learn to judge the pungency of green chili by sniffing a pod.

If fresh green chilies are not available in your area, both canned and frozen green chili can be found in most supermarkets. Green chili is harvested between July and October or November, so finding the fresh pods is not always easy. However, canned and frozen whole green chilies, chopped green chilies, ready-made sauces, reheatable individual dishes and dinners are in the supermarkets to help the busy, working homemaker. Always check the labels to see what degree of pungency you're getting.

Though time consuming, preparing green chilies for use is easy and fun if a few precautions are taken. All chilies, while not full of juice like an orange, are moist and will leave a residue on your hands. Never put your hands near any sensitive skin area, or near the eyes, while handling green chili. If you are preparing one, two or up to a dozen green chilies, a light coating of lard on your hands should be enough to protect them from the pungent juice. If you have a large number of chilies to prepare, I advise investing in a pair of surgical gloves. These fit closely and you maintain the dexterity necessary to work with the chilies.

To prepare your fresh green chilies, lay the pods on a foil-lined cookie sheet, but don't crowd them. Spacing gives you room to turn them, which must be done frequently so they blister evenly. The chilies may brown slightly, but they must be watched so they don't burn. Put the cookie sheet under the broiler (in a gas broiler, use a medium flame; in an electric broiler, turn the element to high) and leave the door open so you can watch and turn the chilies. Remember, you want the chilies to blister, not burn. When blistered and slightly browned, remove the cookie sheet from the broiler. Toss the pods immediately into a bowl or pan of ice water. These chilies will be firm and crisp. If you want your chilies more tender and more thoroughly cooked, remove the cookie sheet from the broiler, cover the blistered chilies with a damp towel and set them aside to steam for an additional 10 to 15 minutes. After steaming, plunge the chilies into ice water. Starting at the "shoulder", peel the outer skin down from the stem-end of the pod and off at the tip. When all your chilies are peeled, you are ready to chop, dice, strip lengthwise, or use them whole.

When you want a very mild chili, slit each pod down one side, spread slightly, and carefully reach inside with your fingers to remove seeds and veins. After this operation, blister and peel as directed.

Another way to blister is to cover a surface unit on your gas or electric stove with a piece of what is called "4 x 4" hardware cloth. Turn your gas flame to medium; electric to high. Place the chilies on the hardware cloth. Watch and turn, turn, turn. When blistered, plunge chilies into ice water and peel as directed. This method is cooler on a hot summer day.

Yes, you can use the hardware cloth over the eyes of your wood-burning stove after the wood has burned down to hot coals. Of course, wood and coal burners won't make this a cool process on a hot summer day. Sorry about that.

I have found there are as many ways to blister chilies as there are people who prepare them. The outdoor grill, after a cookout and while the coals are still hot, is the favored method of one friend. He also disdains gloves, potholders, or mitts, and uses tongs to turn his chilies. Perhaps the best way for working people, who have little or no time to spend preparing fresh green chilies, is to buy those time-savers, the canned and the frozen green chilies.

When you're completely finished and the chili is ready for use, scrub your hands thoroughly. If you used surgical gloves, here are a few instructions that may save you a little time and trouble. Keep the gloves on and wash your hands in lemon juice to remove the chili residue. Rinse, then wash your gloved hands in warm soapy water. Rinse again; dry as well as possible on a towel; dust a little talcum powder or baking soda on the palms and spread it all over the gloves by rubbing your hands together in a washing motion. Remove the gloves by slipping each cuff over the outside of the glove, turning the glove inside out. Blow into each glove, squeeze the cuff to hold the air inside, and check for holes or any damage. If you find the tiniest leak of air, discard the gloves and buy a new pair. Or use lard to coat your hands next time.

If the gloves are still usable, clip them together at the cuff with a spring-type clothespin and hang them in a dark, cool, dry place. Don't ever pull on the fingertips to remove surgical gloves. They are liable to tear or split. After removing the gloves, wash your hands just to be sure no juice has leaked through. Next time you want to slip on your "chili" gloves, the talcum or baking soda will make it an easy operation.

WARNING! No matter how you handle green chili, keep your hands away from your eyes. Chili juice in one's eyes is pure agony. And by the way, don't use or allow your chili gloves to be used for anything except the preparation of chili, and keep those gloves out of the reach of the children.

When a recipe calls for fresh green chilies but you are using canned or frozen green chilies, remember that a 4-ounce can of the chopped green chili is one-half cupful and is equal to approximately three to six fresh chilies, blistered, peeled, and choped. A 4-ounce can of whole green chilies, however, may contain only two to four pods, depending on the size of the chilies. If you do not use all the green chili you have prepared (fresh or otherwise), put the unused chili in a covered dish and refrigerate. If you don't use that chili within two days, throw it out. Better to waste than take a chance. Chili spoils fast and, unlike other foods, the spoilage is not noticeable until too late. So remember--cover, refrigerate, and two days later--OUT!

If you want to can your green chilies for use later after you have blistered and peeled them, USE A PRESSURE CANNER! I use 15 pounds pressure for about one and a half to two hours. (I'm very lax about watching time.) The altitude of your particular area will dictate the time and pounds of pressure you should use. The U.S. Department of Agriculture's Research Service has many good booklets on canning and preserving foods. Write to the Office of Communication, USDA, Washington, D.C. 10150, for their Home and Garden Bulletin No. 8, "Home Canning of Fruits and Vegetables." Include your name, address and ZIP code.

If you have the room in your freezer, freeze your prepared green chilies. You can obtain booklets on freezing food from USDA, too. In using green chili, whether fresh, canned, or frozen, you are limited only by your taste, your imagination, and your daring.

chili

CHAPTER III

Green Chili Salsas and Appetizers

Green chili is an old standby for Southwestern cooks. The table is not completely set if the green chili salsa is not handy to spoon over any and every dish. Friends in Arizona, California, and New Mexico sent me their recipes for green chili salsa. You will notice that all three recipes are basically the same and all three are very simple.

Chili Relish (Uncooked)
(from Arizona)

1 can green chili
1 onion, medium-size
2 tomatoes, medium-size
1/4 teaspoon salt
Dash of pepper

Chop chilies, tomatoes, and onion fairly fine. Season with salt and pepper. Add a little water. Refrigerate in tightly covered container. Good on steaks, etc.

Salsa
(from California)

2 cans green chili, choped fine
2 medium-sized onions, chopped very fine
1 pound firm tomatoes, chopped fine

Combine all ingredients. Add salt to taste. Chill and serve.

Green Chili Salsa
(from New Mexico)

8 to 12 green chilies
1 medium-size ripe tomato
1 small to medium onion
1 clove garlic
1/2 teaspoon salt

Prepare chilies, then chop very fine. Mash garlic in the salt. Blend until almost a liquid. Serve immediately. Make fresh every day.

Let's go into a few extra instructions so newcomers to green chili salsa can get a better picture. You may substitute 1/2 cup of canned or frozen green chili for fresh. Thaw the frozen green chili slightly before chopping. Don't throw out the juice when using canned, whole or chopped green chilies. Drain the juice into the bowl you are going to use for the salsa. Chop the chilies very fine and put them into the bowl. Peel the tomatoes, chop them fine, and add to the chilies. Mash the tomatoes and chilies until almost liquid. Chop the onion as fine as you possibly can; add to the chilies and tomatoes. Stir in the garlic which you have mashed with the salt (and a dash of cider or wine vinegar if you want). Mix thoroughly, or you can use your blender. Always taste a drop before you serve the salsa, to test for pungency.

If you have a very mild salsa and you want a more pungent taste, you can add about 2 tablespoons of cider vinegar. If you are one of the bravest, add finely chopped jalapeño pepper, an exceedingly hot chili with no redeeming features such as mild or medium. The jalapeño is just plain HOT!

For a bit of extra color, use half fresh green chilies and half fresh red chilies (red chilies are ripened green chilies). Prepare the chilies by blistering and peeling, chop fine, but don't use a blender. Let the color show.

If your salsa is too pungent, one tablespoon of olive oil will tone it down a bit. However, if you wish to use the salsa as is, but you want to "cool" it, spoon the salsa over your food, then drizzle honey over all. You'll find your chili is cooler and you have a new and unique taste delight.

Your basic hot salsa can be turned into a sweet but still as-hot-as-like-it salsa by adding 2 tablespoons cider vinegar, 4 tablespoons brown sugar, honey, or molasses, and 1 teaspoon cinnamon.

Hot or sweet-hot, cover your salsa and store in the refrigerator until mealtime. If not consumed at once, these salsas, unlike straight green chili, will keep in the refrigerator for 4 or 5 days, but after that length of time, throw out any leftover salsa and make a fresh supply.

Many years ago I wondered what could be done with an oversupply of milk from my herd of goats. Four growing boys couldn't drink it all up. I hit upon a creamy cheese that had unlimited possibilites--at least, I call it a cheese, my Versatile Cheese.

Versatile Cheese

1 gallon fresh milk (withhold 2 tablespoonfuls)
1 rennet tablet

Heat milk to lukewarm. Remove from heat and add the 2 tablespoonfuls of milk in which you have dissolved the rennet tablet. Cover and let stand until almost solid. Break up the curd and pour into a double-layered cheesecloth bag. Let the whey drain until the bag no longer drips. The curd should be moist, not hard or dry. Dump the drained curd into a bowl. You are now ready to do any and everything with this soft cheese. Yields about 2 to 3 cups.

Scoop out small individual dishes of this cheese; top with fresh, canned, or frozen (thaw, of course) fruit or berries for a dessert. You can mix in wines, liqueurs, spices, vegetables (grated raw, chopped, or mashed-cooked) ground or shredded cooked meats, sliced or mashed fruits, grated cheese, ground nuts, chives, onions, garlic, peanut butter, honey, or you can create anything you want. The combinations can be limited only by you. This cheese is a topping, a dip, a spread, or anything you want it to be.

Avocado Dip

1 ripe avocado, mashed with about
    1 tablespoon grapefruit, lime,
    or lemon juice
1 or 2 tablespoons chopped green
    chili
Dash cayenne pepper
1 cupful Versatile Cheese

Mix all together. Cover and refrigerate for about 2 hours. If still too bland, add more green chili and mix well. Serve with chips.

Remember to taste. Add more green chili if too bland or more cheese if too hot. This next spread can be used as a dip with chips, or you can spread it on crackers or toasted bread rounds. I can tell you it certainly changes a plain bologna sandwish into something else!

Cheese Spread

1/2 cup chopped green chili
1 clove garlic, mashed with 1/2
    teaspoon salt
1 small onion, chopped fine
1/8 teaspoon cumin
2 cups Versatile Cheese

Stir, whip, fold and beat until all is well blended. Cover with plastic wrap and chill for at least 2 hours to allow the flavors to get acquainted.

Always remember to taste. The amount of green chili you used one time may have been perfect, but that same amount can be too much or too little next time. Chilies, whether fresh, frozen, or canned, can be bought labeled mild, medium, and hot. But what happens if the chilies are not labeled? Well, you can breathe easier if everyone cleans up their plates and compliments you on your cooking. Or you can bawl while everyone gasps and staggers off to find something to quench the fire. A pitcher of honey to pour over the food is the best chili quencher I know. Keep one or two pitchers handy on the table always. With at least two pitchers of honey on the table, you won't have to mop up spilled food and honey from floor, table, chairs, walls, and kids. And don't tell the kids they are using too much honey. The hotter the chili, the more lavishly the honey will be used.

During the "good old" Depression days, hamburger, ox-tails, and cheese were either very cheap or free for the asking. What in the world is less than two or three dollars a pound today? Those once-free ox-tails are just slightly less than ground beef, and the prices on cheese are enough to induce cardiac arrest in old-timers like me. If you can find soup bones, pork neck bones, hocks, chicken, rabbit or any meats under a dollar a pound, you have the basis for a good meal. Bone out the cheaper (and usually tougher) cuts of meat and grind your own hamburger.

Before you cuss the butcher for selling you a tough steak, pour lemon juice over or dip the meat in lemon juice, wrap the meat in foil, and refrigerate overnight. If you are wrapping to put meats in the freezer, use lemon juice, wrap, then freeze. You'll find those tougher cuts will be much more tender. This works wonders on older beeves or cows you butcher yourself.

All bones can be boiled to make a delicious stock to use in soups, stews, or almost any recipe that calls for water. Why boil up a mess of beans in plain water when you can use stock to add flavor plus? The marrow in those bones will boil out to enhance the flavor of your stock and will also add surprising amounts of much needed nutrition as well. Use stock and your family will swear you took cooking lessons at a fancy French culinary school!

Nevermore will we see prices as low as they were in the 1930's but cheese is still a good meat substitute. No matter if your recipes range from those ancient years and up to the 1980's, most of those recipes will be enhanced with the addition of green chili. (You thought I'd gotten off the main subject, didn't you? Well, I deviate now and then, but green chili will win out!)

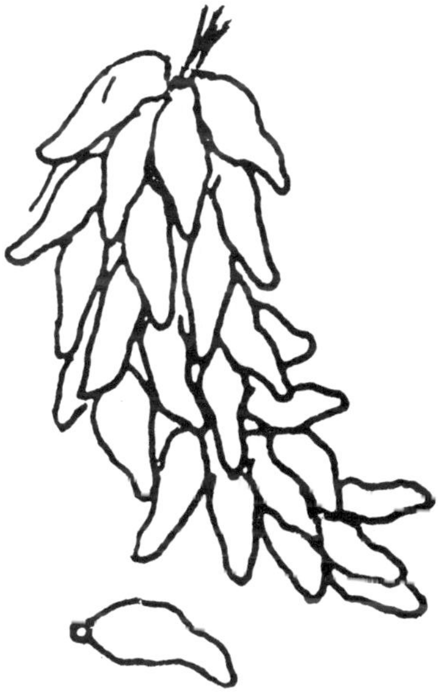

A good Chili con Queso (a sauce much like a fondue) is an outstanding addition to a party buffet. When Connie gave me this recipe, she said, "I've seen people grab a plate, load it up with bread cubes, then pour this con queso over it all. They just scarf it up and come back for more, so maybe five or ten people got in on the first batch. I've had to go back to the kitchen two and three times to make more." I thought she was "plugging" her Chili con Queso until I ran through the same routine. If I want any myself, I have to make this on the sly, then set it out for everyone else as a nice surprise.

Put this into your prettiest fondue pot, keep it warm over an alcohol or candle flame on the buffet, and provide plenty of bread cubes and toothpicks. Or you can set out a big bowl of corn chips for dippping. This may, says Connie, serve about 30 people, but don't count on it!

Connie's Chili con Queso

1/2 cup butter or oil
1/2 medium-sized onion, chopped fine
2 small tomatoes, chopped
1/2 cup green chili, chopped
2 tablespoons flour
1/4 cup water, milk, or cream
1 pound yellow cheese, grated

Over low flame saute the onion in butter until transparent. Don't brown or burn. Sprinkle in the flour and stir thoroughly without browning. Add tomatoes and chili, then add the water, milk, or cream slowly, stirring constantly until slightly thickened. Add cheese and stir until the cheese is completely melted.

These little cheese drops should please those who like snacks they can pick up in their fingers

Chili-Cheese Drops

2 tablespoons butter
3-1/2 tablespoons flour
1/2 teaspoon salt
1/2 cup green chili, chopped
1/2 cup grated yellow cheese
3 eggs, separated
Dash cayenne pepper (or 2 drops tabasco sauce)
Paprika

Melt butter, add flour; stir until well blended. Remove from heat, add salt, chili, cheese, and cayenne or tabasco. Mix thoroughly. Whip the egg whites until stiff. Beat the egg yolks, then pour the sauce slowly into beaten yolks. Now pour this mixture slowly into the stiffly beaten egg whites and fold gently. Drop from the tip of a teaspoon onto a greased cookie sheet, sprinkle with paprika, and bake in a 350° oven about 10 minutes or until just browned.

And how's this for fancy? Set this next recipe in a bowl of ice and let everyone dip. Or you can spread this "caviar" on melba toast rounds or fancy crackers, top with sliced, stuffed green olives or whatever you can think of.

"Caviar"

1 medium-sized eggplant
2 medium-sized onions, finely chopped
3 medium-sized tomatoes, finely chopped
1/2 cup green chili, chopped
2 cloves garlic
1/2 teaspoon salt
2/3 cup olive oil
Salt and pepper to taste

Wash the eggplant, but do not peel. Wrap tightly in foil and bake at 350° about 30 minutes until soft. Chop the tomatoes, onions, and chilies very fine. Crush the garlic with the 1/2 teaspoon salt and mix into the tomato, onion, chili mixture with the oil. Unwrap the eggplant and peel. Chop in small bits. While adding the mixture to the eggplant, continue chopping until all is blended thoroughly and the pieces are about the size of BBs. Chill and serve.

I've said it before and I'll reiterate: You alone limit your imagination. Would you believe this next recipe can be used as a dip, a spread, a salad, or a sauce? Well, just try it and enjoy.

Guacamole

2 ripe avocados, peeled and pitted
2 tablespoons grapefruit, lime, or lemon juice
4 tablespoons chopped green chili
1 thin slice onion, chopped very find
1 clove garlic, mashed in 1/2 teaspoon salt
1/8 teaspoon white pepper

Mash all ingredients with a fork until smooth or use your blender. Serve with taco chips.

If made ahead, smooth a thin layer of mayonnaise over the top of the guacamole; make sure mayonnaise touches sides of bowl to keep air out. Cover with plastic wrap and refrigerate. When ready to serve, mix in the mayonnaise thoroughly.

Place 2 to 4 tablespoonfuls on a bed of shredded lettuce. Garnish with tomato wedges and corn tortilla chips planted decoratively in the guacamole. Or place the tomato wedges on top and ring with chips.

These recipes are just for starters. Add green chili to your marinade, pop in mushrooms, and refrigerate about 2 to 4 hours before serving. Cross thin strips of green chili over the filling on your canapes and hors d'oeuvres. Or make Nachos.

Nachos

On corn tortilla chips place about 1/2 teaspoon green chili salsa. Top with a thin strip of yellow cheese or a little sprinkle of grated yellow cheese. Place under the broiler until cheese is melted. Serve immediately.

You will be amazed at the versatility of green chili once you get into using it.

CHAPTER IV

Green Chili Breads

Green chili in bread? That not only sounds strange; it sounds downright dumb, doesn't it? But just try spicing up your favorite cornbread recipe with 1/2 cup of green chili, chopped. Or try this simple little recipe.

Cornbread

1 cup yellow cornmeal
1 tablespoon sugar or honey
1/2 teaspoon salt
2 tablespoons flour
1 cup boiling water
2 tablespoons shortening
2 eggs, separated
1/4 cup chopped green chili

Mix dry ingredients. Pour boiling water over all, stirring so it doesn't lump. Wet every bit of mixture. If the mix seems dry, add more water by teaspoonfuls. Add shortening so it will melt in the hot mixture. Let the mixture cool before you add the egg yolks and green chili. Whip the whites until stiff and fold into the mixture after you have added yolks and chili. Pour into a small, well-greased pan and bake at 400° about 20 to 25 minutes or until golden brown and a cake tester comes out clean. Serve hot with plenty of butter.

If you are very brave, here's a recipe you might like. I am not a jalapeño person, so I substituted 1/2 cup chopped green chili after my first endeavor. I think I mentioned before that jalapeño chilies are much hotter than green chilies. I do not think you should try this with the jalapeños first to see if you prefer a hot or a milder flavor in your cornbread. It is a more extravagant recipe than the usual cornbread recipes. However, I think you will enjoy this cornbread with jalapeños or with green chili. Give it a whirl at least once. As with any cornbread, serve hot with plenty of butter. A little honey will not only be tasty, but it will also cool those hot jalapeños.

Jalapeño Cornbread

1/2 pound sausage, diced bacon,
 or pork rinds
1/2 cup sifted flour
3 teaspoons baking powder
2 teaspoons sugar or honey
3/4 teaspoon salt
1-1/2 cups cornmeal
1 egg, beaten
3 tablespoons melted butter
3/4 cup buttermilk
1/2 cup canned whole-kernel
 corn, drained
1/4 cup canned jalapeño chili,
 drained and diced
1/4 cup pimientos, diced

Fry sausage, bacon, or pork rinds until crisp; drain and save drippings. Sift flour, baking powder, and sugar (add honey with liquid if not using sugar). Stir in the cornmeal. Combine egg, butter, and buttermilk (and honey if substituting for sugar). Stir into the dry ingredients. Add corn, chili, and fried meat. Mix until just blended; do not overbeat. The batter will be stiff. Pour hot drippings into a 10-inch, cast-iron skillet or a 1-1/2-quart casserole to a depth of 1/8 inch. Spoon in the batter, bake at 400° for 20 to 25 minutes or until a cake tester comes out clean.

Garlic bread, or garlic bread with cheese, is delicious with spaghetti. For a new flavor you might try this next recipe, and maybe you can answer a few questions. Like: What can <u>you</u> do with a plain loaf of French bread? Can you think of other spices to replace the basil? How about a soft cheese to replace the butter?

Herb-Flavored French Loaf

1 loaf French bread
1 tablespoon each parsley, basil,
    green onion tops, green chili
1/2 pound butter

Chop parsley, onion tops, and chili very fine. Combine with basil and butter. Spread on sliced loaf; wrap in two layers of heavy foil; bake in 350° oven for 30 minutes. Serve hot.

Never, for one moment think any recipe is the be-all or end-all of cooking. You can think of new ways to prepare foods, so why depend exclusively on others to dictate what you cook and eat?

TORTILLAS

You've heard of tortillas, haven't you? You have probably seen and possibly tasted them—just flat rounds that look easy to make. And they are. Flour tortillas are great with any chili dish, beans, or almost anything. But did you know you can also make sopaipillas with the same recipe as for flour tortillas? Sopaipillas, you know are those little puffy pillows that can be stuffed with meat, beans, or anything else you wish, or you can cover them with sugar and cinnamon, or pour a little honey inside. You can serve them as a main dish or a dessert. Just because I wanted to I have included a recipe for flour tortillas from scratch.

Flour Tortillas

5 cups flour
1 tablespoon baking powder
3 tablespoons lard
1-1/2 to 1-3/4 cups hot water
1-1/2 teaspoons salt

Combine dry ingredients; cut in lard. Add hot water while kneading thoroughly. Dough should be stiff but not sticky. Roll about 1/2 cup of dough into a very thin circle. Do not use flour when rolling out. (Roll between two pieces of plastic wrap and save your temper). Bake on a very hot greased griddle until browned lightly on both sides.

Divide the dough in half and instead of making only tortillas, roll half the dough to about 1/4 inch thick in a rectangle. Cut into 3 inch squares and fry in deep fat until light brown and puffed, turning once. Drain on paper towels, then roll in a mixture of 1/2 cup sugar and 1 teaspoon cinnamon. Or serve plain with a pitcher of honey. Just break in half and pour in some honey. Super-delicious! Or slice one end open and stuff with beans, cooked meat, cheese, sour cream, guacamole--just another recipe that calls for your imagaination.

The Quaker Oats Company puts out Masa Harina Instant Mix to make corn tortilla making even more simple and easy. The directions are on the package, but I'll include them here.

Corn Tortillas

2 cups Masa Harina Instant Mix
1 cup plus 2 tablespoons water

Combine Masa Harina and water. Mix until dough forms a ball. If necessary, 1 or 2 teaspoons more water may be added. Shape into 14 to 16 balls and cover to keep dough from drying out. Place a ball between two pieces of plastic wrap and roll out to a 6-inch circle. Or use a tortilla press if you have one. Carefully peel off the plastic and bake dough on an ungreased skillet for 30 seconds. Turn and bake the other side for 1 minute. Turn again and bake 15 to 30 seconds. Tortillas should be soft and pliable, not hard or crisp.

To make your own tortilla chips, cut the tortillas in quarters before baking. Quickly fry the triangles in deep fat for a few minutes until chips are lightly browned. Scoop out and drain well on paper towels. Salt lightly and serve hot or cold with dips, soups, salads, chili con carne, beans, etc.

Burritos can be made with your flour tortillas, and those little tacos can be made with your corn tortillas. Look for the packages of Masa Harina for corn tortillas and Masa Trigo for flour tortillas. Both these Instant Mixes are made by the Quaker Oats Company for quick and easy tortillas. They should be found in your supermarket. And they are perfect aids for the working homemaker.

CHAPTER V

Green Chili Main Dishes

Imagination, testing, tasting, and experimenting, plus daring, while caring for their families' nutritional needs brings everyday cooks to the brink of artistry. Some teeter on the edge, then pull back, afraid of what people may say or afraid of failure. Others plunge straight on and come up with innovations that tantalize—and failures that fall far short of hopes and expectations. If every cook turned back because of one failure, we would still be eating raw meat and gnawing on old bones. Instead, we have recipes that the timid can use and take their bows; the bold will embellish those same recipes with the array of spices that call for experimentation and blending, with the vegetables and fruits from every part of the world, and with green chili, of course.

Hamburger, cheese, and the so-called cheaper cuts of meat can be used with imagination to cut food bills, but no matter how you prepare foods, green chili can add zest as well as titillating new tastes.

Albondigas spell meat balls in Spanish. Yes, it's as simple as that. The mainstay of one country, sometimes with slight variations, is the mainstay of many countries. Have you ever considered that meat balls are tiny meat loaves? Open your eyes and see things in a different light now and then. Enliven those weary taste buds. Put some bite in every bite. Whether you serve only yourself or a dozen, make everyone glad they sat down at your table. The following recipes are merely to whet your appetite for invention and innovation.

Albondigas

1 pound hamburger
1/4 cup cornmeal (white or yellow)
1 egg
1 clove garlic, minced
1 small onion, minced
1-1/4 teaspoons salt
1/4 cup green chili, chopped
1/2 teaspoon pepper

Mix all ingredients thoroughly. Shape into balls about 1/2 inch in diameter. Make a sauce as follows:

1 tablespoon drippings
1 small onion, chopped
1 clove garlic
1/2 teaspoon salt
1/4 cup green chili, chopped
1 tablespoon red chili powder
3 cups tomato juice

Melt fat in a large saucepan. Add onion and cook slowly until lightly browned. Add garlic, chili, chili powder, and tomato juice. Boil for 10 minutes. Drop hamburger balls into boiling sauce. Cover and simmer for 5 to 7 minutes. Serves 3 or 4.

Substitute tomato paste, sauce, or puree and water or stock. Try adding different spices; whip up your favorite spaghetti sauce and drop the meat balls in to cook. Serve with rice or potatoes, a green vegetable, salad, and green chili salsa on the side.

You can thicken the sauce with a little flour; you can make a meat loaf instead of meat balls and bake for an hour to an hour and a half at 350°.

Beans

Have you noticed that one simple recipe can take on different shapes, tastes, and colors? Well, look at the lowly dried bean (also dried peas and lentils). In fact, look in any cookbook and you'll find so many recipes showing you how to fix dried legumes that I won't go into the basics, except to suggest that you use stock, whenever you can, rather than plain water. Pinto beans are the favorite fruit in New Mexico and most of the Southwest. After cooking the beans, what can be done to make them more interesting? You can add salt pork, pork rinds, necks, hocks, bacon, sausage, ham, shredded cooked pork or diced pork. But how about hamburger, shredded or diced beef, chicken, rabbit, or even venison? Squirrel, cottontail, or jackrabbit are tasty additions that cook up tender when added early on and simmered with the beans long and slowly. Jazz things up with onions, celery, garlic, green chili, tomatoes, a little oregano, savory, tumeric, sage, or other spices. Too much liquid in your beans? Thicken with a little flour, or just try 1/2 to 1 cup of yellow cheese.

When cooking beans, I try to think of what I can do to make the plain very unplain. I have had what might be called a bean stew--meat, potatoes, tomatoes, carrots, celery, Bell pepper, green chili (of course), and beans. I have also used dried peas and lentils this way. I have made green chili con carne and added the beans to that. I have used sage, savory, marjoram, tumeric, basil, oregano, peppercorns (whole and cracked), or other spices--either alone or wildly mixed up. No matter if the beans are plain or all gussied up, I serve them with cornbread or tortillas, plenty of butter, and plenty of honey.

Refried Beans

2 cups dried beans, cook in
stock or water and salt

Drain the bean juice into another pan. Mix into the beans about 1/2 cup lard, bacon grease, or oil. Over low heat, stirring constantly, simmer about 25 to 30 minutes while adding a little of the bean juice and mashing the beans lightly. No, don't mash the beans as you would potatoes. Some of the beans should look as if they were just cut in half. Continue adding a little of the juice and mashing the beans gently until a thickened gravy appears. Remove from heat and serve as a side dish with grated yellow cheese melted on top.

I realize there are those in this world who wouldn't touch beans for anything in this world. Beans are just for those prosaic people like me who love them despite their faults. Or should I say their fluency? Beans certainly will talk back to you now and then!

Let's say you've boiled up a pot of pintos (or other variety of bean). Let's also say you put nothing in the beans except salt. Already you're on your way to refried beans, burritos, and any number of other bean dishes.

If you're looking for a main dish on one plate, get your heavy skillet or your griddle and heat it to 400°. Toss on those flour tortillas, whip them off onto a warm plate. Get your refried beans, green chili con carne, the grated cheese, chopped onions, shredded lettuce, and tomato wedges ready at hand and you're in business. All set? Let's make burritos!

Burritos

Spread 3 to 4 heaping tablespoonfuls of refried beans in the middle of a warm flour tortilla. Sprinkle chopped raw onion on the beans. Roll up, place on a warm plate or platter, lavish green chili con carne over the burrito, dress up with grated yellow cheese on top of the burrito, and surround with shredded lettuce and tomato wedges.

That's just a plain bean burrito. Mix beans and meat; beans and avocado; beans and sour cream; beans, meat, avocado and sour cream; meat alone; meat and other vegetables; fruit; all of the above; or you think of something. Just roll your creation inside a flour tortilla and you have a burrito. Just don't forget the green chili!

You know, the first burrito I ever bit into was a tightly rolled flour tortilla dipped in hot green chili sauce. That was a New Mexico burrito, filled with beans, meats, or combinations--a burrito that is a full meal you can serve for lunch or dinner. You can see that the other areas of the West and Southwest use the same name for rather different foods or different ways of fixing practically the same foods. I don't know all the differences and I don't know all the ways foods can be prepared. I doubt that one person could try every possible mixture and method, even if that person lived to be 1,000 years old. So I am giving you a few recipes that hopefully will stimulate your own desire to test, taste, and experiment.

Let's make a great pie for lunch or just a light supper. I have baked Quiche Lorraine with and without green chili and compliments wafted around my ballooned head. This Chili-Cheese Pie is similar to Quiche, yet it is slightly different. I, of course, accepted the compliments for it, too. In this pie you may use Swiss Cheese if you wish, but any cheese can be used--jack, cheddar, gouda, whatever you might like. You might have bits of different kinds of cheese. Go ahead and mix 'em! They'll blend and bring out new tastes. Be a little daring now and then.

Chili-Cheese Pie

1 unbaked 9-inch pie shell
4 tablespoons butter
4 tablespoons flour
2 cups stock (milk may be substituted
1 lemon, juice and grated rind
1 pound jack, cheddar, or other cheese, diced
4 eggs, separated
1/2 to 1 cup green chili
4 to 8 tablespoons grated cheese for topping

Bake pie shell for 10 minutes at 400°. The shell should be faintly tanned and slightly underdone. Melt butter in a pan over low heat. Add flour and stir until well mixed but not brown. Add stock, lemon juice and grated rind slowly and stir until thick. Add a pinch of salt and stir in the diced cheese. When cheese is melted, remove pan from heat. Whip the whites into stiff peaks; set aside. Beat the yolks slightly, add a little of the sauce to the yolks, beating constantly. Stir green chili into the sauce in the pan, then add the yolks to the sauce, stirring constantly. When well mixed, fold sauce into the stiffly beaten egg whites. When whites and sauce are well mixed but still fluffy, pour into the partially baked pie shell. Sprinkle grated cheese over the top and bake at 400° about 10 or 15 minutes. The pie should be puffed and browned, not burned. Serve with a big tossed salad.

Four to six slices of bacon, fried crisp, drained, and crumbled, may be added.

Saute 1/2 cup finely chopped onions in the butter before adding flour.

Use tart shells instead of one 9-inch pie shell.

What else can you think of? What would you like to add or replace with something else or leave out? Do you buy a cookbook and read it from cover to cover? Or do you skim through and pick out just the things you know? Have you studied recipes that seem similar? Do you break down those recipes to the basic ingredients to see what has been changed, what has been added, what has been replaced. Well, come on! Get with it and delve into those books. They look so lovely on the shelf, don't they? I'll clue you. They are gorgeous inside. They read better than some best selling novels, too. And cookbooks are far more stimulating!

How about a casserole? This one can be dressed up with so many other things--hamburger, tomatoes, Bell peppers, and on and on, or you can serve it exactly as is and still accept deserving compliments. Line your casserole with pie crust before filling; make changes like standing thick tomato slices on end instead of layering within the mixture; slice and quarter tomatoes and mix into the chili-corn combination. Need I go on? Take it from there and see what you can come up with.

Chili-Corn Casserole

1 tablespoon butter
2 tablespoons flour
1 cup stock or milk
1/2 teaspoon salt
2 eggs, slightly beaten
1 No. 2 can whole kernel corn
(drain and use liquid as
part of stock or milk)
1 cup soft bread crumbs
1/2 cup chopped green chili
1/2 pound yellow cheese, sliced,
diced, or grated

Melt butter; stir in flour. Gradually add stock or milk. Stirring constantly, cook until mixture boils and thickens. Add salt, corn, chili, and crumbs. Slowly pour a little into eggs to warm them, then mix into the eggs thoroughly. Layer 1/3 of mixture into a greased casserole, cover with a layer of cheese, add another layer of chili-corn; a layer of cheese; the last layer of chili-corn. Cracker crumbs may be sprinkled on top, then melted butter poured over. Bake in a 350° oven for 45 minutes to 1 hour.

Casserole Variation:

Parboil Bell peppers for 5 minutes; drain and stuff with chili-corn mixture. Cross slices of cheese over the tops, or you can mix the cheese into the chili-corn. Pour tomato sauce over all and bake at 350° for about 1 hour.

Remember that I am only trying to give you a little push. Please don't take any recipe given here as an absolute. You will have inspirations of your own that may make my recipes look like feeble attempts to cook. Believe me, I won't mind that at all. I would rather you enjoy cooking and thinking of new ways to enrich and enhance the food you serve your families and guests. I don't believe all recipes must be followed exactly. If you have an idea of your own, try it. Just throw in some green chili for good measure.

For this next recipe you should have fresh green chilies, roasted and peeled, with the stems left on. Canned whole green chilies don't work too well because they are not firm enough and they have no stems. However, canned whole green chilies are better than no Chili Rellenos at all.

Chili Rellenos can be baked as a casserole or you can substitute other things instead of using cheese. Imagination and daring are the keywords again and yet again. Let's give it a try.

Chili Rellenos

6 fresh green chilies, blistered and peeled
1/2 pound block of jack cheese
1 onion, finely chopped

Depending on the size of the block of cheese, cut in strips about 3 to 6 inches long and 1/2-inch wide. Cut a small slit just below the stem of each chili. Stuff very carefully with cheese and onion. Do not split or break the chili. Holding by stem, dip each chili into batter.

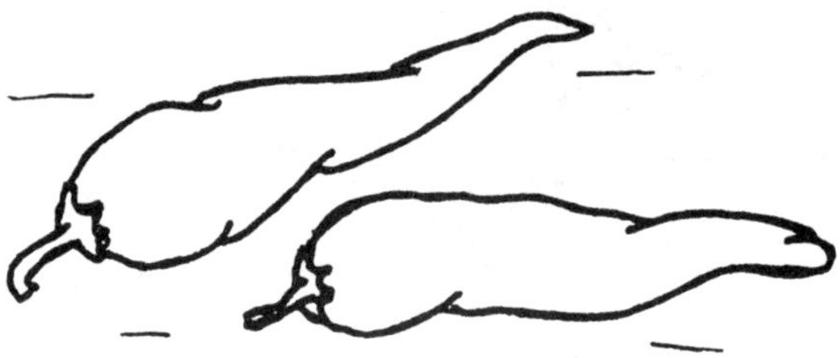

Batter

4 eggs, separated
4 tablespoons flour
3/4 teaspoon baking powder
1/4 teaspoon salt

Beat whites until stiff; beat yolks until thick. Sift dry ingredients. Fold yolks into whites; add dry ingredients and blend well. Dip stuffed chilies into batter (a large spoon helps). Fry in a small amount of fat, turning once. Place rellenos on a serving plate and hold in a warm oven until all chilies are cooked.

Or dip chilies, lay in a baking dish, and pour batter over all. Bake for 45 minutes at 325° until batter is set and slightly browned on top. Serve at once.

Substitute well-seasoned, cooked, ground or shredded meat, for the cheese stuffing.

Huevos Rancheros

I have cooked scrambled eggs in the top of a double-boiler over hot water, in a sauce pan, in a frying pan, on a griddle, on gas and electric ranges, on wood-burning ranges, old box heaters, in fireplaces. I have even used a pie plate over a camp fire when I forgot my cast-iron skillet. What you cook in or on isn't the most important item. What you cook and how you embellish the recipe should be uppermost in your mind. What can you do besides toss scrambled (or fried over-easy, sunnyside-up or however) eggs on a plate with bacon, ham, sausage, toast, and hash-browns? Well, the plate can be garnished with tomatoes, parsley, strips of green chili, green chili salsa, or a host of other things.

You can mix in chopped green chili as you beat the eggs for scrambling. Along with the green chili you can add chopped tomatoes; or saute chopped Bell pepper until slightly tender, and chopped onions and saute until both are done. Pour eggs into the pan, add green chili and some chopped tomatoes; cook until eggs are done to your liking. A little grated or diced cheese may also be added.

Or you can pour eggs into the pan and let them cook slowly until set; don't stir or scramble them. When set, put green chili, tomato, sauteed Bell pepper and onion, and grated cheese on one half. Cut down the middle and fold the other half over. Slice into two, three or four wedges and serve. Cooked bacon, crumbled, can be added. Or stir-fry sausage (or hamburger) until done and add.

Cook flour tortillas, place on plates, then place two fried eggs on the tortillas for each serving. Now pour green chili con carne over the eggs. Serve Huevos Rancheros immediately.

You can see what I mean? Sure, plain scrambled eggs are good. Just a little imagination and a few additions can make them fit to serve guests for lunch or even for supper when you haven't enough chops or steaks or beans to go around. Never be afraid to dress up and add to recipes. I have added barley, rice, noodles, spaghetti, or macaroni or beans to extend and cover the unexpected. A couple of fried or poached eggs can be amazingly tasty when strips of green chili are daintily placed on top.

Fish

Most fish is bland, but it needn't be. Dredge a freshly caught fish with cornmeal or flour, fry it over your camp fire, serve with green chili (whole, strips or chopped), fried potatoes, fresh-baked biscuits, and maybe fresh tomato slices, too. Your camp buddies will think you have suddenly turned into a gourmet cook.

The air turns blue when I mention carp to my fishermen friends. I think they just hate to scale and clean them. It is a chore, I'll grant you, but a large carp that gave you a good fight before you reeled him in deserves better than to be tossed into the brush. Carp are bony little devils, too, but you have to watch out for bones in any fish. If you detest carp, you can substitute any fish in this recipe.

Baked Carp with Green Chili

1 large carp, scaled, cleaned, boned, and filleted
6 strips bacon
4 green chilies, blistered, peeled, and sliced lengthwise
3 medium-sized tomatoes
1 medium-sized onion
1 cup sour cream (wine may be substituted)
1 cup margerine, melted
1 tablespoon paprika
Salt to taste

Lay one fillet in baking pan. Alternate strips of bacon and green chili over the fillet. Slice tomates and onions thin and lay over bacon and green chili. Cover with second fillet and sprinkle with salt and the paprika. Pour over all the melted butter and the sour cream (or wine). Bake in moderate over at 350° until fish is tender; baste frequently with liquid in baking dish. Serves 4 to 6, but do be careful of the bones!

Flank Steak

Once I was told never to buy flank steak because no matter how you cooked it you wouldn't be able to eat it. My curiosity was aroused to such heights that I had to see for myself. I am pleased to report that I have not served a tough flank steak in 40 years. Back in the 1940's I used a saucer to pound the flour into my steak. I graduated to a mallet, but I much prefer using the thick edge of a heavy chef's knife to break down the fibers. One thing to remember is that you must pound the steak to almost double its original size. I must warn you that this method takes two days; so you should plan ahead, buy the steak(s), work them up, then refrigerate overnight. The stuffing can be made ahead and refrigerated, or you can do that job on the day you will be serving the steak. Choose the method that is easiest for you.

Flank Steak

2 flank steaks, each 1 or more pounds
Flour
Salt and pepper
2 cloves garlic, minced
1 lemon
1 cup red wine

Dust a board with flour; lay one flank steak on floured board; dust with flour, salt, pepper, and half of the minced garlic. Pound steak to about double its original size, turning steak over several times. When flour, garlic, salt, and pepper are pounded into the meat, and both flank steaks are beaten to submission, grate the lemon rind into a dish; cut lemon in half and squeeze juice through a strainer onto each steak. Roll each steak up very tightly, place in a baking pan, pour the wine over the steaks, and sprinkle the grated lemon rind on top. Cover closely with foil and refrigerate overnight.

Stuffing

2 cups dried bread crumbs or cubes
1/3 cup butter
1 onion, chopped
1 stalks celery with tops,
  chopped fine
1/2 cup chopped green chili
1/2 teaspoon sage
1/2 teaspoon marjoram
1 can tomato sauce

Lightly brown onion in butter; pour over bread. Add celery, chili, and spices. Mix with enough wine from the baking dish to hold stuffing together. Lay steaks on a board and spread stuffing over each. Roll up with steaks and skewer or tie with string. Any stuffing that falls out may be tossed into the baking pan. Return the rolled steaks to the baking pan. Pour the tomato sauce over the steaks, then fill the can with wine (or half wine, half water, or all water); add to the sauce in the baking pan. Also add any stuffing left in the bowl. Cover with foil; refrigerate until about 3 hours before you plan to serve. Preheat oven to 350° and bake the steaks for about 2 hours, covered with the foil. Remove the foil and bake about 10 to 20 minutes longer. Cut into about 1-inch slices. Depending on appetites, you might be able to serve 4 or 6.

Lasagne

Lasagne may be Italian, but you can give it a Southwestern flavor by adding about 1/2 cup of green chili to your sauce. You can do the same with spaghetti and other pastas. Why anyone wants to put the same dishes on the table every night with no change in the tastes, I don't know, but many people do just that. I don't mean to imply that you should use green chili in everything everyday. That would be as bad as a menu of boiled meat, boiled cabbage, boiled potatoes, and boiled carrots every night. That even sounds tiresome, doesn't it? I mean, it not only sounds tiresome to eat every night of your life, but it sounds tiresome to prepare, too. A good boiled dinner can be plain and taste just great without spices or green chili. Perhaps one or two weeks later you can serve up your boiled dinner with additions to liven palates with an entirely different taste. You can have the same dishes, but you don't have to have the same flavor every time. The cook's imagination is what keeps the taste buds tickled and the family busily cleaning up plateful of nutritious food without thoughts of posing that horrible question: Not (whatever) again?

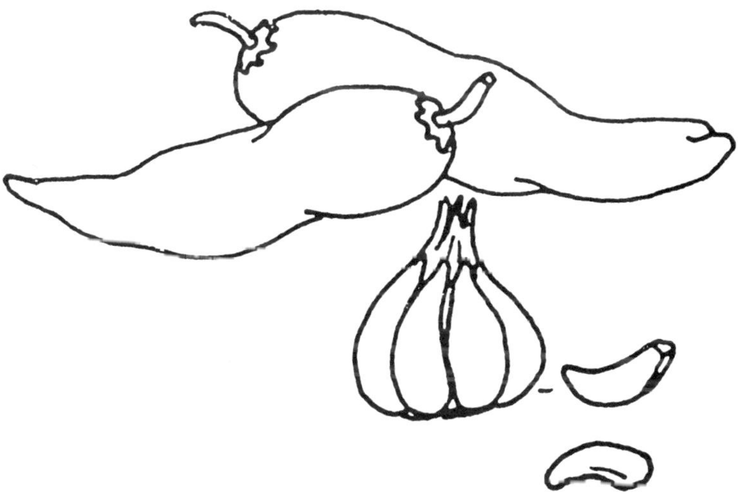

Chili con Carne is best known as red. However, Green Chili con Carne is, I think much more versatile. Some like it plain; some like it hot. The cook decides the pungency preferred.

Green Chili con Carne

1 pound lean meat, cut into 1/2-inch cubes
2 tablespoons lard
2 tablespoons flour
1/2 cup chopped onion
1 clove garlic minced
2 cups coarsely chopped tomatoes
1-1/2 cups chopped green chili
1/4 teaspoon oregano
1-1/2 teaspoons salt
2 cups water

Dredge meat in flour. Melt lard in a deep skillet or Dutch oven and brown meat. Add onions and garlic; cook until onion is soft and yellow. Add remaining ingredients and simmer, covered, about 2 hours. Remove the cover and simmer about 5 to 10 minutes to desired consistency. Serve in bowls with tortillas, crackers, or chips.

Add 2 cups cooked pinto beans.

Use as a sauce over burritos, Huevos Rancheros, or other dishes.

Pork is preferred for Green Chili con Carne, but rabbit, chicken, hamburger, beef, mutton, venison, game animals, game birds, turkey or any meat has been used successfully and, I might add, the con carne was excellent. Many-a-hunter, I know, packs all the ingredients in his old Dutch oven, then hunts down a jackrabbit, a cottontail, or a few quail. While the wife, or some poor guy who gets tricked into staying at camp, watches and feeds the fire, the con carne stews for hours. By the time everyone is back in camp, with or without deer or other game, the chili is ready to eat. The hotter the chili the less problem one has staying warm in the New Mexico high country during the cold fall and winter nights.

Certainly, you can throw in potatoes, carrots, celery, or anything else you can think of to make a green chili stew. Just because the recipe is labeled Green Chili con Carne, doesn't mean you have to stop there if you have ideas popping into your head as fast as bullets from an old 1930s gangland Tommy-gun. Get busy and try 'em. You could pleasantly surprise yourself--and you don't have to wait for the fall and winter hunting seasons. I don't recommend hunting summer rabbits. They are a bit scrawny and usually pretty well tick and flea-infested. Buy rabbit, poultry, or the cheaper cuts of meat at your market and try your ideas in your own kitchen. Or you may find that you have something stashed in your freezer that you can use.

I wasn't going too deeply into Mexican cooking, but some of the Mexican recipes, such as Green Chili Enchiladas are so easy that I shall give you my recipe.

Green Chili Enchiladas

1 cup green chilies, chopped fine
1 medium onion, chopped
1 cup chopped tomatoes
1 tablespoon fat
1/2 cup milk or sweet cream
Salt to taste
6 corn tortillas
1 cup grated yellow cheese
Shredded lettuce
Tomato wedges

Saute onions in fat; add tomatoes and chilies. Add milk or cream gradually, stirring constantly. Simmer about 5 minutes. Fry the tortillas in 1/2 inch of fat in a heavy skillet. Turn once. The tortillas should be soft, not crisp, if you are going to roll them.

Roll tortilla around a stuffing of cheese or sour cream or lightly mashed cooked pinto beans or cooked meat, or combine any or all to create your own stuffing. Pour green chili salsa or con carne over the rolled enchiladas, garnish with shredded lettuce, tomato wedges, and sprinkle grated cheese over all.

Flat Enchiladas

Lay one corn tortilla flat on a plate. Spread with stuffing of your choice, spoon over some of the salsa or the con carne. Stack on the second tortilla; spread with the same or a different stuffing; spoon sauce over. Do the same with a third tortilla. After spooning over more sauce, garnich with lettuce, tomato, cheese, and if desired, a fried egg can be placed on top of these flat enchiladas.

Now you take it from there—and test, taste, and experiment. You can buy or bake a round loaf of bread, slice it in rounds from the side rather than from the top, toast the slices lightly and use in place of tortillas. I don't think pumpernickel bread would work too well, but then I have never tried it in place of tortillas.

This recipe is a custard, but don't try to use it for a dessert! Sweet it is not. It is great as a luncheon dish with a big tossed green salad. This is another recipe that just begs for you to try out your imagination. See what you can dream up to enliven and improve the basic recipe. I think you'll be glad you did.

Green Chili Custard

- 5 slices of bread
- 1 tablespoon oil or butter
- 1 cup grated cheese
- 1/2 cup stuffed green olives, sliced
- 3 eggs, slightly beaten
- 1/2 cup green chili, chopped fine
- 1/8 teaspoon dry mustard
- 1/3 cup of the olive liquid
- 2 cups milk, scalded

Cut the crusts off the bread slices, dry the crusts slowly in the oven. Roll the dried crusts into crumbs and set aside. Spread the bread slices with 1 tablespoon of oil or butter, stack, and cut into cubes. Scatter 1/2 of the cubes over the bottom of a greased baking dish or a casserole. Add a layer of about 1/2 of the cheese, chili, and olives over the cubes; add another layer of about 1/2 of the remaining cubes, another layer of cheese, chili, and olives, but withhold about 1/3 cup of the cheese for topping. Cover with the remaining bread cubes and dot with butter. Combine the eggs, mustard, and olive liquid. Add hot milk gradually, stirring constantly. Pour over the layers in the baking dish, sprinkle the toasted crumbs over the top, then sprinkle the remaining cheese over all. Bake about 1 hour in a 300° oven, or until a knife inserted in the middle of the custard comes out clean. This should serve 6.

Tacos

12 corn tortillas

Fry the tortillas in about 1/2 inch of hot fat. When just softened, fold tortilla in half. Fry until crisp on one folded side, then turn and crisp the other side. Drain on paper towels and set the shells upright in a pan. Put the pan in a 200° oven to keep warm. When all shells are fried, fill each with the following:

Filling

1 pound ground meat, browned in 1 tablespoon oil
1 clove garlic, minced
1 small onion, chopped
1 cup chopped tomatoes
1/2 cup chopped green chili
1/4 teaspoon each salt, pepper, oregano, and cumin
2 cups shredded lettuce
1 cup grated yellow cheese

Put garlic, onion, chili, and seasonings in a saucepan and cook for about 25 minutes. Add the browned meat. Fill taco shells with 2 or 3 tablespoons of the meat filling. Now sprinkle on some shredded lettuce over the filling, add some chopped tomatoes, top with grated cheese. For those who like it hot, pour about one tablespoon of green chili salsa or con carne cross the top.

Beef, pork, chicken, rabbit, mutton, venison, turkey, game—any meat may be ground or shredded to use as taco filling.

Beans can be mashed and mixed with the browned meat filling.

Raw onions may be chopped and sprinkled over the filling—or chopped green onion tops may be substituted.

Tostadas

This recipe came from California and has been a favorite with everyone because I prepare everything, then set bowlsful out so they can fix their tostadas as they wish. When I say tostadas to New Mexicans, they think I am going to serve corn tortilla chips. Same words, different foods! Confusing, but that's life when you mix the West and the Southwest, and then throw in a little of Mexico and Texas, too. No, not confusing—it'll purely drive you crazy trying to keep everything straight!

Bertie's Tostadas(for 4)

1 pound hamburger, fried well-done but not crisp
1 to 2 cups green chili salsa
1 cup cooked pinto beans, mashed while reheating
4 corn tortillas, heated in a heavy skillet
1 cup grated yellow cheese
1 cup chopped green onion, tops and bulbs
1 head lettuce, shredded
4 or 5 tomatoes, chopped
1 or 2 cans chopped ripe olives
2 or 3 ripe avocados, diced, then dipped in lemon juice
1 to 2 cups sour cream.

Place warm tortilla on the plate first. In the middle put a big spoonful of beans, ring with hamburger; ladle on a bit of salsa; sprinkle a little cheese, onion, lettuce, tomato, olives, avocado and more salsa; top with sour cream and a bit more salsa.

This is how the tostada should be built, but some people will decide they can do without the beans or the onions or something else. Each individual creates his own tostada and enjoys the process. I have chopped Bell peppers and set them out, too. Not a smidge of anything was left! But don't take my word. Try it yourself. Oh, I should advise you that this is great eating out-of-doors. If you plan to have it inside, set up your buffet, but let your guests eat at the dining table. Avocado, cheese, beans, sour cream, tomatoes, etc. wreck havoc when stomped into carpets or spilled over and down the insides of chairs.

How would you like to put a little kick into pigs' feet or knuckles? Just add a little (about 1/4 to 1/2 cup) green chili. I love 'em plain, but that chili puts a punch into pigs' knuckles that can't be beat.

Pigs' Knuckles

5 medium-sized knuckles (about 3 pounds)
2 medium-sized onions
2 large bay leaves
6 sprigs celery tops
1/4 to 1/2 cup green chili, chopped
1 clove of garlic, crushed
1/8 teaspoon each thyme, allspice, sage
3 whole cloves
8 peppercorns, bruised
1 teaspoons salt.

Scald knuckles in boiling water, scrub with a brush in lukewarm water, and remove any hairs by singeing. Place knuckles in a stew pot with water to cover to 1 inch above knuckles. Add all other ingredients and slowly bring to a boil. Boil 5 minutes. Reduce heat; simmer, covered, for 2 hours, skimming occasionally. When meat is ready to fall from the bones, lift out knuckles and drain well. (Strain the broth and save for a soup stock.)
Serve with red cabbage or sauerkraut and steamed potatoes.
Serves 5 to 6.

CHAPTER VI

Green Chili Salads, Sauces, & Stuffings

Did you think I would leave you in the lurch as far as salads were concerned? Or did you think green chili was impossible to add to a salad? Well, look through your cookbooks at the variety of salads and consider which ones might be punched up with maybe one tablespoonful of chopped green chili. Perhaps you'd like to try a bit in a dressing. You'll never know unless you try it.

One of the easiest salads to make and one that allows you to experiment readily is cole slaw. I don't know all the ways cooks have dressed up the commonplace head of raw cabbage—pineapple, grated carrots, sugar, honey, vinegar, lemon juice—I could list more, but that would be a book in itself.

Cole Slaw

1 large head of cabbage
1/3 cup vinegar, (cider, white, or tarragon)
1 tablespoon honey
1/2 teaspoon salt
Dash each pepper and paprika
1/4 cup green chili, minced
1 tablespoon pimiento, minced
1/4 cup mayonnaise
1/4 cup yogurt, sour cream, or cottage cheese

Shred cabbage and soak in ice water for 30 minutes. Drain and dry thoroughly. Put vinegar, honey, salt, pepper, and paprika in a large bowl; add cabbage, toss to dampen; let marinate for an hour. Drain and squeeze cabbage slightly to remove excess moisture. Pour the marinade into a smaller bowl and add the green chili and pimiento. Let this stand while you mix the yogurt, sour cream, or cottage cheese with the mayonnaise. Add the marinated bits of pimiento and chili to the mayonnaise. If you want a thinner type dressing, add a little of the marinade until you have the consistency you desire. Pour over the cabbage, mix thoroughly, and serve.

Now, here's a way to remove the bland label from cottage cheese salads.

Green Chili-Cottage Cheese Salad

1 cup cottage cheese
1/4 cup mayonnaise or salad dressing
1/4 cup finely chopped green chili
1/4 cup finely chopped onion
1/4 cup finely grated carrots

Mix all ingredients thoroughly. Serve on a bed of lettuce, garnish with tomato slices or wedges and a sprig of parsley. Dust lightly with paprika.

Or try this variation:

Slice off tops of 4 medium-sized tomatoes, scoop out pulp carefully. (Save the pulp: You can use it in your salsa.) Fill the cups with chili-cottage cheese mixture, dust with paprika, set on beds of lettuce and serve.

Aspic salads lend themselves to the additon of green chili, as this recipe will show you.

Green Chili-Ham Aspic

1-1/2 tablespoons unflavored gelatin
1/2 cup cold water
3 cups tomato juice
Dash of salt
1/2 bay leaf
1 to 2 tablespoons finely chopped onion
1/2 cup finely chopped green chili
3 cups minced baked or boiled ham (other meats can be substituted)

Soften gelatin in cold water. Combine tomato juice, salt, bay leaf, and onion in a saucepan; simmer for 10 minutes. Strain, add gelatin and let cool. Mix the green chili with the ham (or other meat); add to gelatin, pour into mold and chill until set.

Unmold and serve.

You may have had better luck than I have had with dipping a mold into hot water to loosen the gelatin when unmolding. I have found that letting my hand-held drier heat just to warm and waving it over the inverted mold drops the gelatin after maybe two or three passes. Any sign of liquid running onto the plate from the inverted mold should tell you the mold is too warm. If you continue warming it, you may have to mop the floor.

Sauces

A good hot sauce for meats that can really steam your ears will depend on how much green chili you use and the pungency of the green chili. This recipe is fairly mild, but as I have said before, test, taste, and experiment to find the degree you want.

Green Chili Meat Sauce

1 can whole green chilies
1/2 cup oil
1 clove garlic, mashed in 1/2 teaspoon salt
1/4 cup cider vinegar

Mix all ingredients except the chilies. Lay the chilies in a bowl; pour the sauce over them. Refrigerate to blend the flavors, about 2 to 4 hours. Serve chilies whole or slice in strips to top roasts or steaks. Spoon on a little of the sauce, too.

Pork Ribs

You should know that pork ribs don't have to be barbecued. You can stuff them with a basic bread stuffing, a cornbread stuffing, or just bake them in a bed of sauerkraut. Most people have a favorite stuffing. I am no exception. I love cornbread stuffing, but I detest giblets in any stuffing. If you have never used green chili in stuffing, it is simply fabulous in anything that can be stuffed--turkey, chicken, rabbit, game hens--anything. Any cookbook will have a recipe for basic bread stuffing, and many also tell you of other ingredients you can add to the basic recipe. For my Pork Ribs with Sage Stuffing I reduced my recipe to half the amount I would use for a big turkey, and because pork is a fatty meat, I omitted the lard, oil, butter, or fat that I would normally use. I have used cornbread in place of white or wheat bread and added many different things at various times. Just because the recipe is staring at you from a printed page doesn't make it a sacred cow that you must do nothing with but follow meekly. You can, and you should add, adjust, subtract, replace, or make almost any recipe suit you and your family. Give your own ideas a chance.

Pork Ribs with Sage Stuffing

1 rack pork ribs about 1-1/2 feet long, or 2 smaller racks, each about 8 to 10 inches long

If you have one large rack, cut it in half. Lay one half in a baking pan so the hollow can be filled. When filled, lay the second half on top so the mounded stuffing fits into the hollow area.

Sage Stuffing

2 cups dry bread or cornbread
1 onion, chopped fine
1 egg
1 cup water, stock, or wine
1/2 cup green chili, chopped
1 tablespoon sage
1/2 teaspoon poultry seasoning
1 teaspoon salt
1/4 teaspoon pepper

Saute onion in a very little oil until tender. Drain. Combine all ingredients thoroughly. Fill the rib hollow with the stuffing, cover with the second rack, and pour 1/2 cup wine or apple juice over the ribs. Core, but do not peel 6 or 8 red apples; quarter the apples and drop the pieces around the ribs. Cover and bake at 350° for 2 hours. Uncover and bake 1/2 hour longer.

You may ring the ribs with sauerkraut or sauerkraut and apples.

Have you ever stuffed a meat loaf? After mixing it up, pat the mixture into a rectangle, spread stuffing on top, roll up, tuck the ends under, then bake as you would any meat loaf. I know you have ideas of your own. Try them even if they seem strange and far out. Your imagination is as good as (if not better than) mine.

A basic bread stuffing can be changed by any particular addition or combination of additions. Green chili goes well with your basic stuffing or with the additions you choose. I will give you my basic bread stuffing, then I will follow that with a short list of things you can add. You can grab the ball and run it yourself.

Basic Bread Stuffing
(For 8 to 10 lb. fowl)

4 cups bread or cornbread,
  crumbs, cubes, or crumbled
2 cups water or stock
1/4 cup melted fat
1 teaspoon salt
1/4 teaspoon pepper

Combine all ingredients. You may want to add an egg. Stuff bird, but allow room for expansion.

Now, what can you add? Green chili, for starters, at least 1/2 cup. In the list that follows, you can add one, some, or all of these items.

1 cup chopped apples
1/2 cup chopped green chili
1 cup minced celery, tops and stalks
3/4 cup chopped mushrooms
1/4 to 1/2 cup chopped onion
1 to 6 teaspoons sage
1/4 cup chopped parsley
1 cup coarsely ground nuts
1/4 cup chopped Bell pepper
1 to 3 teaspoons of savory, thyme,
  marjoram, poultry seasoning,
  oregano, or any other spices
  you wish—alone or in combination

Yes, if you so desire, you may add giblets—plus anything else you can think of. Raisins, rice, barley, potatoes, wheat, carrots, fruits—there are so many things that can be added that I can't begin to list them all. Whatever you add, make sure you add the green chili to your stuffing!

CHAPTER VII

Green Chili Vegetables

I haven't said much about what green chili can do to your vegetables, have I? Well, here's your chance to test, taste, and experiment. To get your ideas gyrating, look in your cookbook for recipes for the vegetables you plan to prepare. While thinking "Green Chili", consider other ways to enhance those vegetables. The following recipe is not too well-known nor is it used as frequently as it might be, but if you like onions, you may enjoy it.

Apple-Onion Scallop

9 medium-sized onions
6 medium-sized cooking apples
12 slices bacon, cut in small pieces
1/4 cup green chili, chopped
3/4 teaspoon salt
1 cup water or stock
1/2 cup buttered bread crumbs

Peel onions and apples; slice about 1/8-inch thick. Fry the bacon until crisp; drain on paper towels. Grease a casserole, now alternate layers of onions, apples, bacon, and chili. Sprinkle with salt, add water or stock, top with crumbs, cover and bake at 375° for 45 minutes. Uncover and let crumbs brown slightly for another 15 minutes. Bacon fat may be used in place of butter on the bread crumbs. Serves 6.

Don't just put a bowl of corn on the table. Gussy it up a bit; you guessed it, with green chili.

Mexicali Corn

3 cups whole-kernel corn, canned, fresh, or frozen
1 onion, minced fine
1/2 cup chopped green chili, (or whole chilies cut into strips)
1/4 cup pimiento, diced
Salt to taste
1 tablespoon oil

Saute onion in oil until golden. Add all other ingredients. Stir constantly and heat thoroughly over low heat. Frozen whole-kernel corn may take more time to heat through.

Green Bean Casserole

1 cup brown sugar
1 cup catsup
1 tablespoon minced onion
1/4 cup chopped green chili
3 to 4 pieces bacon
1 No. 2 can or 2 cups cooked green beans
Salt and Pepper to taste.

Brown bacon until crisp. Mix the other ingredients in a casserole Pour bacon drippings and crumbled bacon over green beans. Blend well. Bake in 350° oven for 25 to 30 minutes.

Have you ever taken a covered dish to a potluck party where the first few dived in and cleaned it up completely? Then have you listened while those few exclaimed over it, but everyone else found only the empty dish? Aggravating, isn't it? I felt good about the compliments, but I felt bad at the same time because I had not made more. This last recipe I have doubled and redoubled in the hope there would be enough for everyone. Although this should serve 5 or 6 people, I no longer bank on it—especially at a potluck party! It is a fact of life that when the food is free, you'll find there are those who will load up their plates with huge amounts of everything. You just have to be prepared.

This next recipe is one some people refuse to believe because they have never even heard of Jeruselem artichokes, those funny, knobby little tubers that are delicious substitutes for potatoes.

Jeruselem Artichokes

1-1/2 pounds firm Jeruselem
    artichokes
1/4 to 1/2 cup finely chopped
    green chili
1 small clove garlic, mashed in
    1/4 teaspoon salt
Salt, pepper, and butter to taste

Scrub artichokes; cook, covered, in boiling, salted water for about 30 minutes or until tender. Do not overcook because tubers will become tough. Drain; strip off outer skin. Mash or put peeled tubers through a potato ricer with the garlic, chili, salt, and pepper. Mix butter into artichokes lightly; serve with a pat of butter on top. Sprinkle a teaspoon of chopped parsley over the butter and artichokes for color.

For something better known, add a clove of garlic to the water with your potatoes. Boil until tender, drain the water, and mash your potatoes with 1/4 cup green chili. Add milk, butter, and salt. Whip again and serve. And you know that rice is also an excellent change from potatoes, too.

Rice and Green Chili

2 to 4 cups cooked rice
1 cup sour cream or yogurt
3 tablespoons chopped chives
1/2 cup chopped green chili
1/4 cup butter or margerine

Mix sour cream or yogurt with chives about 1 hour before you wish to serve this dish. Let stand at room temperature. Heat rice if already cooked, or boil enough to measure the amount you desire. Add butter to hot cooked rice; mix well. Add green chili and the chive mixture. Simmer very gently over low heat until all is warmed thoroughly. Serve at once.

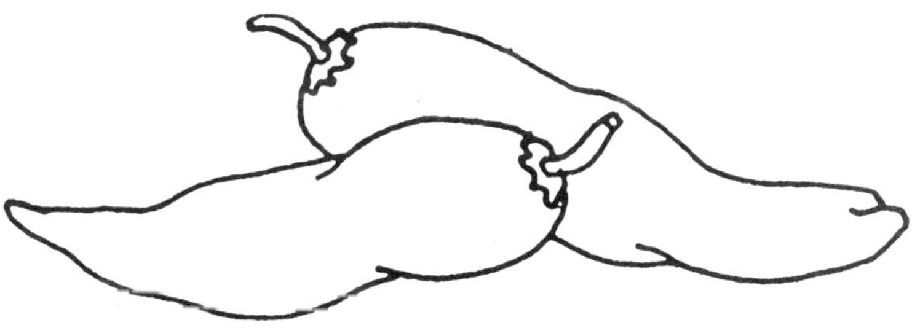

Did you grow an overabundance of squash in your garden? Did you have to throw away what you couldn't give away? But you say you have dozens of jars of beautifully canned squash? That's wonderful. Whether banana, acorn, scallop, zucchini, or any other kind of squash, you can use some of your oversupply. Those who can't grow a garden will have to buy whatever squash is available in the market, but all of you--get ready for a new taste in squash.

Squash with Green Chili

2 cups squash, cubes (any kind will do)
1 tablespoon fat
1 small onion
1/2 cup chopped green chili
1 cup fresh or frozen corn

Saute onion in the fat until limp Add squash cubes (or slices if you prefer—cut about 1/4-inch thick), the corn, and the chili. Cook slowly with very little or no water until squash is tender. Salt to taste. Serves 5 or 6

Now, do you think these are all the ways to fix vegetables? Are these the only recipes in which you can use green chili? Perish that thought immediately. I have given you just a few recipes so you can stir up your own ideas. I've said it before and I'll say it again: These recipes are simply for starters for you to get your mind in gear. I don't want you to depend on this booklet or to imagine that it contains all the recipes that you can use. A cookbook that encompassed all the recipes in which you can use green chili would run into hundreds of pages--and probably would not cover all the possibilities.

As you read over your larger, more comprehensive cookbooks, consider each recipe carefully. How would green chili go with baked carrots? Or stewed tomatoes? Or—must I go on? I want you to have the excitement of discovering the pleasures of testing, tasting, and experimenting with green chili.

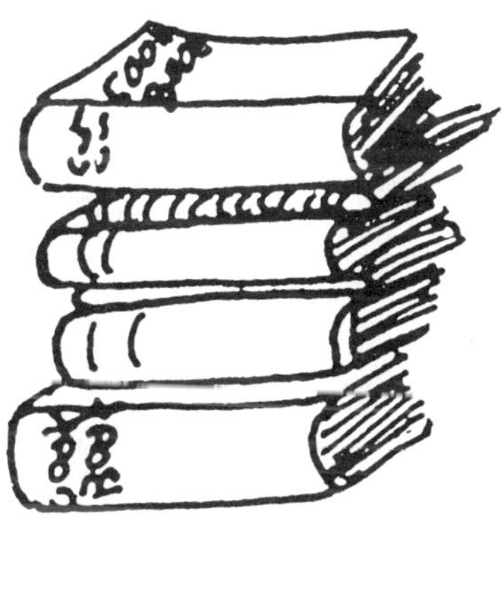

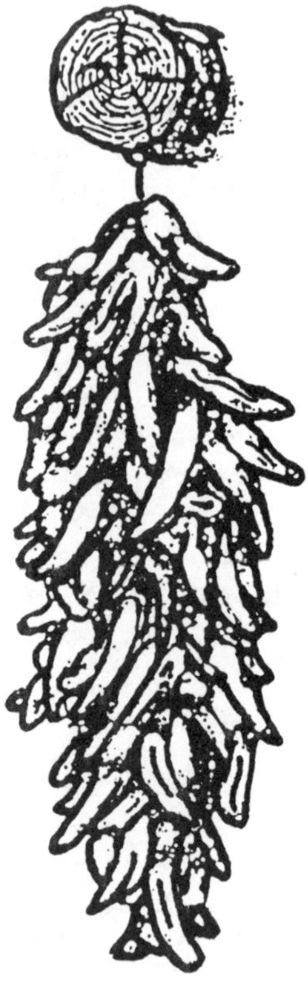

CHAPTER VIII

Finale

You now have a small idea of what can be done with green chili. If I thought you needed a full-fledged cookbook devoted entirely to every possible recipe in which you could use green chili, I would have tried to give you just that. I don't like to think that you have no mind of your own and need everything spelled out in black and white, step by detailed step. I may be an idealist, but I do believe wholeheartedly that you who read this booklet and want to try green chili will do so. I am also sure that you will test, taste, and experiment as exuberantly as I have.

Believe me, I have had plenty of fiascos. I think everyone has followed a cake or biscuit recipe down the line, word for word. What happened? The cake fell or it didn't rise at all. The biscuits were only good for pelting stray dogs. Did that stop you? Or did you want to try again, but backed off from a cake and baked a pie instead? Did the crust turn out like a shoe sole? Your loaf of bread didn't rise even a smidgen? So you now depend on the packaged mixes and you've sworn never to try "from scratch" again?

You may have tried something that was a perfect recipe for sea-level, but did you ever consider that altitude can make a big difference? Water boils at a lower temperature at higher altitudes. So what can you do about it? Talk to your County Extension Agent. Write or call your State Agricultural College or Department. Every State and County has a research unit that can help you discover why certain things went wrong. You can even talk to the Home Economist at your Public Service or Gas Company. You'll be amazed at the work these people have put into research in your area just to help you prepare foods more economically and more tastily.

It's time to "get off the dime" and really serve your family nutritional foods. Nutritional does not have to mean imitation soybean steaks or ground-up earthworms plus additives no one can pronounce—much less spell. If you grow your own food and bring it in right from the garden, you don't want to undercook or overcook or add things in which the ingredients are questionable. You want the fresh taste and all the natural elements you can possibly keep in those fruits and vegetables. If you do add something, you want to be sure you are adding vitamins and minerals as good and pure as possible. When you add green chili, you are adding the natural and pure vitamins A and C, not mile-long chemical names.

Admittedly, I do not put green chili in every dish I set on the table. I think that would not only be foolish, but it would blunt appetites. Sometimes I serve no green chili dishes at all—except for the green chili salsa which everyone can use or leave alone as they choose. I will leave the menus for your family up to you. If you wish to add green chili to one of those dishes, I think that's great. If you have merely read through this little booklet and have no intention of trying green chili in anything at anytime, I think that's great, too. My sincere hope is that you have enjoyed reading this wee booklet as much as I have enjoyed writing it.

I have tried to show you what possibilities there are for green chili, but I would much, much rather find out that you have tested, tasted, and experimented with all foods and that you have envolved new and different dishes to present to your families, with or without green chili.

Now, get into that kitchen and cook up a storm. If you are a working person, you may have to rely on the canned and packaged foods because you have little time or because you are too tired to bother. Remember, though, that you won't always have to dash off to work, dash home, and make like a whirlwind in the kitchen. When the time comes, you can take more time, relax, and cnjoy cooking. Who knows? Someday you may be cooking for your grandchildren. Feed 'em well!

INDEX

MORE GREEN CHILI RECIPES

MORE GREEN CHILI RECIPES

MORE GREEN CHILI RECIPES

MORE GREEN CHILI RECIPES